HEADLESS
JOHN THE BAPTIST
HITCHHIKING

HEADLESS JOHN THE BAPTIST HITCHHIKING

POEMS

C. T. SALAZAR

ACRE
CINCINNATI 2022

Acre Books is made possible by the support of the Robert and Adele Schiff Foundation and the Department of English at the University of Cincinnati.

ISBN-13 (pbk) 978-1-946724-48-9
ISBN-13 (ebook) 978-1-946724-49-6

Designed by Barbara Neely Bourgoyne
Cover art: USGS topographical map of the Mississippi River. Unsplash.

The press is based at the University of Cincinnati, Department of English and Comparative Literature, McMicken Hall, Room 248, PO Box 210069, Cincinnati, OH, 45221–0069.

Acre Books books may be purchased at a discount for educational use. For information please email business@acre-books.com.

for Carlos & Haley Salazar

CONTENTS

I

Sonnet for the Barbed Wire Wrapped around This Book 3
All the Bones at the Bottom of the Rio Grande 4
Portrait of the Dalmatian That Bit My Mother 6
My Father in the ICU 8
Traveler but I Scarcely Ever Listened 10
When the Crows Came 12
Saint Toribio Romo of Guadalajara Finally Stopped Praying 13
Triptych Just before Mass 14
Barnburner 17
Mostly I'd Like to Be a Spiderweb 18

II

Parable about Changing My Name + an Elegy 21
It's Easy to Become King of a Place No One Wants to Live in 23
Shades of Red 25
Six Ecclesiastical Love Songs 26
Poem with the Head of Homer in It 29
The Mouse Speaks 30
If a Star, Break This Elegy into Its Blossoming Fingers 31
Incident Number to Be Determined 32
Forgive Yourself for Seeing It Wrong 33

III

Sonnet River 37
Self-Portrait as Headless John the Baptist Hitchhiking 42
Love, Circular Saw Blade 43

After Us, the Flood 44

Noah's Nameless Wife Sees a Golden Bust of Joan of Arc 45

As Long as You Want 46

Poem Ending with Abraham's Suffering 48

Ode 50

IV

You Called Me Castaway and I Called You 53

Palinode, or Lullaby with Light and Dark 54

Novenas 57

Noah's Nameless Wife Takes Inventory 60

You Are Counting the Waves 61

All That Dazzling Dawn Has Put Asunder: You Gather a Lamb 62

Poem with Three Names of God + a Promise to Myself 63

NOTES 67

ACKNOWLEDGMENTS 69

SONNET FOR THE BARBED WIRE WRAPPED AROUND THIS BOOK

You were the first to show me what my blood
looked like + praise be the first to say no
to my soft body + sharp apology +
I know your name by heart: NO TRESPASSING
you tight metal fist + glory your afterkiss
I saw you barbed on Christ's bleeding head
+ knew heaven speckled us like cattle
like I could be a wound cruxing a field

+ come dawn I'm a saint blue parable
so telling how paradise takes + takes
+ maybe I wanted the world to wrap
around me regardless of what that meant
+ on my arms these torn constellations
made me heaven + my chest of bright stars

stick up like a cradle growing out of the mud. All the bones at the bottom
of the Rio Grande know the same song but cannot

sing. They raise the river, but only a little, as when Archimedes lowered
the gold crown into the bath to study displacement. Displacement: *noun*.

The moving of something from its place. All the bones at the bottom of
the Rio Crande know this definition. To replace with oneself what would

otherwise be occupied with fluid. To be as much the river as
the river—all the bones at the bottom of the Rio Grande have changed

      their name to Rio Grande. The Rio Grande has so many names.
            Río Bravo del Norte: Great River of the North, or Hanapakwa
        in the Towa, or boundary or border to the desperate, or my love
            I swear I'll come back for you. In between two halves of me
          a river is running. I've named that river Rio Grande.

That river named me survivor, named me *lucky*. Is there a word
for the opposite of a miracle? There must be a sound. Punctured whistle

of air leaving the raft. All the bones at the bottom of the Rio Grande
needed a home more than they needed a lifeboat. All the bones at the

bottom of the Rio Grande I've inherited the way my mother inherited
my grandmother's teapots. I've seen two shatter. They fell with no river

      to catch them. Is ruin by land a sweeter heirloom?
      Imagine to be gone. Record   destroyed. Archimedes's book
        of handwritten mathematics a thirteenth-century monk erased
      page after page and filled with prayers to the Lord. All the bones
      at the bottom of the Rio Grande rattle at the word *erased*.

All the bones at the bottom of the Rio Grande have finally found
a place willing to make room for them, and all the bones

at the bottom of the Rio Grande will reverse this river when
their children call.

PORTRAIT OF THE DALMATIAN THAT BIT MY MOTHER

Because someone forgot to lock that fence.
Because of all the shapes, I came in the shape

    of rage. Because I carry July

in my skin. Because every pair of hands handles me
violently. Because my mouth is most my beastliness.

Because Grendel must have also hated chains—
        must have also howled at the tall silhouettes.

    Because the birds looked

the other way but weren't troubled enough to flee. Because
the thigh was pincushion soft and seemed defenseless

    as an abandoned beehive.

Because I didn't think her hands could hold so much
    survival. Because

    her son was nearby.

Because *No—dumb dog, I'll kill you if you don't get away
from my child.* Because he is still tender. Because

    the antonym of bite is kiss and she kisses him

        every day. Because

    breaking   the skin   of a mother

only means   putting your mouth

to a muscle that tightens   a universe

of danger into a single soon-to-snap
harp string.

MY FATHER IN THE ICU

He says   the IV needle is long
like a dragonfly   with torn-
off wing   what would you
call this?   not the dragonfly
but the way   I didn't realize I'd
be strong enough   to lift his
gray body, his hair   flat from
sweat, his arm   outstretched
like Adam exiled   from the
Sistine Chapel, Adam with a bad
gallbladder and IV   dripping
morphine. I would call   this
acceptance of defeat and   I
would call   the skin under his
eyes the grave   where his pride
is buried   I wake up and he
is a cloud   floating above
the bed. I rub my eyes until he's
a man   again saying my shoes
need a good polishing and that
he'd do that   for me when he
gets out of this place,   where
his body   is as messy   as
his handwriting.   He is a bear
they cannot manage.   He is
a handful   he is an arkful.
Surgeons removed a glassy-eyed
fish   choking on a rosary bead.
Yes, he is a bear rubbing smooth
my heart walls   as he lumbers
back and forth from conscious
-ness. I rub my eyes with hands
the color of burnt   clay pots

I make a jar with them   I tell him
Look, daddy,   even your grief
is not too heavy   for me to hold

TRAVELER BUT I SCARCELY EVER LISTENED

Shoot me & I'll explode   into feathers   my mother says

I'm soft but the truth is   when I say I'm sorry I mean

I'm sinking   sorry sir   did you know

the Liberty Bell weighs 2,080 pounds   so heavy

it cracked itself   have you ever dreamed

of that kind of freedom   the sacrifice of sound

say to yourself   it's an honor to break

for my song   my pioneer   I have been on the bad side

of every priest I've ever known   so says the Lord anyone

with a forked tongue is trespassing this garden   some moons

are made entirely out of dust particles   floating together

this is how I talk about my family   how you

could reach a hand straight through us   a ghost

you could wave away   my pioneer   it's cold in America

& no one taught me the names of your constellations

so I named them after mi familia   & what they did

to survive   look above us there's   Abuela Ojos Estrellados

& Tío Mario   his crown of shooting stars   the constellation

guiding me   America   is a pile of glimmering shovels

WHEN THE CROWS CAME

I didn't hate them.   They needed to roost
and I needed a purple deep enough to con
-vince the neighborhood boys   of my

skin's milkiness.   I don't mind   seeing
strands of my hair in their nests—   pages
of scripture I've torn out,   strips of silver

chocolate wrappers,   stray threads
from old sweaters, they take it all, curious
gods.   The young ones chirp.   Every

morning my body's outlined   in feathers,
the whole bed   dappled dark
as a beginning.   I don't know what to say,

so I say thank you. The crows don't know
what to say, so they don't speak, they just
keep finding parts   of me to make useful.

I thank them for that too.

SAINT TORIBIO ROMO OF GUADALAJARA FINALLY STOPPED PRAYING

when they shot him *Here I am*
say it when you're covered in dirt
like a priest deep in the bowels
we know we're men because
our angels don't recognize us
our bodies fissured by black
Lord believe me I've tried
but the desert could hold its breath
Saint Toribio Romo's prayer is
the empty rifle shells
of his last morning
you'll learn not to turn from
the name that slithers around
don't let the catacombs frighten you
the skull seems sinister but
that could be your uncle
it's hard to tell bones apart
or any ancestor of yours really

aquí estoy   but do not kill me
like a dog lost in damp corridors
of some factory   Yes
our wars outlive us
and our children bury
bullets   each wound a mouth singing
to suffer the drought
a little longer   remember
how forgiveness gathers inside
the exit wounds
how siblings hold us when we're dead
the bones that build your heritage
in your hands
any relic left behind is a miracle
that could be your father
if it has the right bullet hole
almost every saint has them
you all look so similar

TRIPTYCH JUST BEFORE MASS

for Franz Wright

I

We stood in the shape of an open jaw, the piano

our black tongue, and breaking out of the room's teeth
a multitude of carved horses, which is just another

way of saying I stood with my hand over my mouth

     when the man wrapped in dirty blankets approached
     the piano and started playing twinkle

twinkle little star.

II

Always the awe   in hacksawed.
Always the word *sanctuary* to shave down

like sweet lemon peels. A child broke the stained glass
window once. The next day he left it

reassembled on the floor, as if we could look through
and see our precious saints chewing termite-rich roots.

III

Christ on the wall reminds me of the tree
the field raised after lightning burned it white

with new knowledge. If God is cold it's because
he left the nursing home with only a few

      dirty blankets and muddy socks. If God speaks
      it is in single syllables we board like boats

      to reach our fathers.   Yes   if God speaks
      it is a single golden O like Saturn's largest ring.

BARNBURNER

The barn doesn't love you, though over and over you enter

its wide mouth like Jonah passing back and forth through the fish.

Even with four horses and a loft full of crows, the barn is of no mind.

The smoke above the barn is just the sky   remembering

the barn. Say it. Say the flame inside is just the barn pretending

to be a man. The next time you put faith in anything, remember when

the wind blows, the barn sings   until it runs out of breath.

MOSTLY I'D LIKE TO BE A SPIDER WEB

because in the rain I'd look like a cracked window
without a church to belong to. You could look

      through me and see the world in front of us.

One time, my ex-lovers made a road of tongues for me.
I took my shoes off to feel the song a little better

and cut a note short with each step.

I want to tell you how many churches
I've built to praise little things that deserve
more than their few seconds of existence.

Like the time I opened my door, smelled hibiscus,
      and knew you were home.

      Like the time a child told me there was a god,
      and because he was smiling, I believed him.

Mostly, I'd like to be a spider web to feel you walk through.
To see if you'll take me with you, despite the spider I bring.

PARABLE ABOUT CHANGING MY NAME + AN ELEGY

The cotton field on fire looks like sunflowers, somehow
caught between praise and persecution. Field of saints

aflame. Horizon gone godless, the sky black
with devotion. The prophets knew the body had to break

to become part of God's alphabet. How the O
in the middle of *devotion* looks like a gunshot

through a bird too colorful to be native.
How heat withers the leaves to curled surrender.

When I change my name this time, it's Abednego—
it's the boy whose greatest miracle was not needing

an apology from the burner. Abednego, the body.
Foreigner to the furnace. If I am too colorful to be native.

If my smoke is sweet. Quémame, inherited name.
Quémame, blood in the restless shape

of my family. Quémame, second tongue
I keep in my mouth.

+

Come cracked, come crawling cobblestone, come
with enough to drag yourself through this old drought

with its new name. Come alive. Come break
the dishes of the dead. Come, but you can't stay

because there is no vessel for you to weep into anymore.
Because all day I've had to pretend you're not

the dried-out moth stuck in the hymnal. Come call me
your teacup. Your copper coffee ring you left sitting

on the windowsill. Come in the hours my mother
has flowers in her hair. Come watch her pull long-stemmed

miracles from behind her ear, and bring the vase
she needs. Come lilies, lilacs, lifetimes

of petals on the dining-room table. Come willing
to look the afternoon in the eyes, the blue shape

of pity. Come cloud.
Come pregnant with rain.

IT'S EASY TO BECOME KING OF A PLACE
NO ONE WANTS TO LIVE IN

—but it's really hard to stay alive after that.
There is what is real and there is what will be

real, and this logic beheads me over
and over.   I named the scarecrow Ozymandias.

I think of my insides as strange aquariums for
little blue fish when I'm falling asleep. I said I'm sick

of you, but I meant to say I'm seasick of you—
rain is usually the first sign a curse has ended

but it means so little to my family's drought-dry
bones. Still the sky says Nonbeliever, hinge open

your jaw for me,   the star-filled star-
field.   Here I believe no country like the country

where you and I for the mercy of the barn bending
into the meadow bend back and demand

a life this dirt could never really give us.
That's okay. This was a language I was never meant

to speak, but here I am   speaking it. Like a paper
tiger unfolding in a field, I am waiting

to be unrecognizable: how could I love you
in one single shape? Any crease made by your hands

makes me a treasure map. I'm a temple bell when
you ring me.   The moth with the orange eyes of God

blinking on its wings sees us and sees
us soldiers not knowing what to do with

ourselves or especially our hands on a night
so absent of fire so faith in something

like resting my head on your shoulder comes
easy as the atmosphere spending

its sweet time on us, even with so many
stars bumping their foreheads against the glass. Even

with your hands holding my head together and you
singing about surrender and the men who won't.

SHADES OF RED

red giant   red blood cell see the difference
is not carbon just its patience   the question
turns from brick red   what have you been building
to rust red   how long have you been building it

I danced in a barn my grandfather built with a girl
who told me we used to be stars and maybe the stars
remember   ruby   I felt valuable   desire

is a shade of red   crimson   crimson I
didn't wear any   tiptoeing a barn rafter I tripped
hot red cheeks and hysterical laughter   rename me

blush   rename me rose

SIX ECCLESIASTICAL LOVE SONGS

heaven is a compound
word
      the sun sunders
us dazzling
so you don't have to
wonder what wound
I'm showing

    :::

    heaven-heavy

    a cello's hello—

       / heaven-heavy

    like an animal fond of its own

    fur

       :::

       A cello's hollow
       that's what it felt like

       breathing with you
       in the dark

:::

heaven is a compound

      but not the one we're in

we were called heathens in another myth
hello   whatever wound we answer to now

:::

the language of electricity was
      the language of prophets

a conduit for the power to pass through
      I'm all steeple at your lightning

let us tremble cellos
      at your touch

    :::

      the river knowing which way to go

      without any godspeed to spill

      heaven: clouds marigolding softly

:::

birds drones butterflies a jug

      of water   anything

could get over that fence

POEM WITH THE HEAD OF HOMER IN IT

The list of relics is long / and I want to find everything I've lost
I understand we're constantly losing things / and this makes them

valuable / the bones of Saint Peter / didn't you know / were found
recently / Peter knew where they were of course but the wisdom

of the dead is mostly lost / on us / good only for gathering dust but
somewhere there must still exist the remains of people / who may

or may not love us today / if they could / the world we're withering /
if Homer was real he loved wine / he would've loved me / and all my

flightless magnificence / if Homer was blind all those marble sculptures
of his face could see as much as he could / this makes him the perfect

subject / are you still with me / what if I've lost my way / stumbled
into this coffin called home / this may or may not be my country

the American dream and me have little in common / we will
both be dead / in no time / relics someone might find / if they dig

the marble head of Homer / probably doesn't remember its home
or its body / forgetting is a kind of mercy / eventually even the cemetery

forgets it is a cemetery and looks like an open field / one Homer
would've loved for a battlefield / one Odysseus could ask

his son to carry him across / there's more than one kind of battle
I tell myself these things / as if it'll stop me turning to stone / my country

cracking me / imagine me buried in a cemetery that forgets it's a cemetery
relics in a field / my belt buckle / my father's watch / his name engraved on it

THE MOUSE SPEAKS
for T. K. Lee

I burrow   I wiggle   I chew through
the pulpit and through the dead   don't you see
that which you call sacred I have tasted   your

fathers brought me here in their ships   their coat pockets
my eyes shining like stars in the man-made dark
you wouldn't think me starlike but   a star

is only as big as the god   whose black skin
it shines against don't you see   I live

by not being   running in the parasol's moving shadow
step on me it's fine   I have brothers   they don't
have names either just my body   and my bite

but really whose hunger brought us here

IF A STAR, BREAK THIS ELEGY INTO ITS BLOSSOMING FINGERS

If a star, lullaby up and down freely.
If a star, love me from a reasonable distance.

If a star, a scar glimmering.
If a star, hydrangea me blue.

If a star, swallow me first.
If a star, carve.

If a star, crave me lonely.
If a star, swirl with gorgon eyes.

If a star, look with crackling mirrors.
If a star, give God this hydrangea.

If a star, cosmos me laughing.
If a star, smear me light.

INCIDENT NUMBER TO BE DETERMINED
after a drowning

A savior who forgot to come up

after his baptism—maybe that's who the man was.

What would you have saved us from? Who were you
talking to for so long down there?

I can't pull a man from the water

     and not think of birth.

What would you have become if we left you—
a tectonic plate? It doesn't matter

     how many questions you ask him,
     he answers in mouthfuls of tadpoles.

Wring the hair dry. What would you have saved us from?

The river is dirty. I am sorry this was all we could
give you. I would have given you the ocean:

starfish to hold you and angelfish to kiss
your blue lips.

Some shore we could all stand on and mourn,
never having known you. The crabs, their claws in the air,

would have wept too.

FORGIVE YOURSELF FOR SEEING IT WRONG

under the rosequartz clouds even a man glimmers

like a bride his hatchet a bouquet   I am waiting

for his tears to turn pearl   ache and its flag

of unfurling twilight   the telephone wires make a strange harp

over our heads and if we weren't here who

would talk about heaven   root-ridden and a little afraid

of the notion that light has a tendency to keep going

like my father on his motorcycle   maybe I've spent too much

time listening to the distant rain on the rooftops of people who may

kill each other and believed it's not too late for me

to make this about love   the man in the field and his farmtruck

even now I hear him his voice such a split of lark and lemon

this crooked intimacy how the last train mixes its smoke with the dusk

and the cattle bed down around the chevy   taking it

as one of their own   light sinking unable to chime and helpless to touch

SONNET RIVER

Everything in the house will catch fire,
if you can believe that. Mississippi
burns you last if it loves you, and now all
your neighbors keep an ax in the house.
A dog on a chain means some angers you
can own but never trust, tricycle child.
The sound of a bell means someone wants you
to answer the door. Don't keep them waiting.

Baby, I'll be your bullet-peppered stop
sign—your steady aim and your favorite
smear of stars to shoot at. Bounce a bullet
off a church bell. If the ringing reaches
God, he'll bless our names: call us his children
of King James and Remington: lightning bolt.

;;;

Of King James and Remington, lightning, bolt
action—all of these can fill the body
with new knowledge. In some gospels, God's grace
gets lost before it gets here, and hardens
from a river into a rattlesnake:
I press every cow skull to my chest
looking for that holy hum. I whistle
to dead birds but no miracle happens.

Every eulogy with the river
involved proves how hungry our river
grows each season. Season of broken neck.
Season of derailed train dangling from
the railroad bridge. And so says the river:
This is plenty. This is more than enough.

;;;

This is plenty—this is more than enough
field to follow your shadow into shape
-lessness. Surely it's a blessing to leave
the light and not feel lonely. You undress
me of my apologies and say I
look better without them. You know me best
beneath the dark river of stars: the spools
of barbed wire dragging across heaven.

After Adam was buried, Eve begged God
to let her keep some part of her husband,
so God dropped Adam's new heart in her hands.
She couldn't believe how heavy it was.
The children cried when they saw it gleaming—
in this telling, God called the heart *Ax head*.

;;;

In this telling, God called the heart *Ax head
cleaved deep in the body's bark.* My body
dark as the moon's inside. November's jaw
bridled to the cold. Crickets crushed under
horse hooves and my belief the next life
will need their little song for intervals
between falling toward softer light. Please keep
your hand in my hair as long as you want.

You in the field. You holding my father's
revolver, heavy as a handshake. What
war is waiting for us to lie down long
enough to forget our names? Every
bullet will be fired in due time. Love,
every belief grows teeth to chew you.

;;;

Every belief grows teeth to chew you
tenderly. If you ever feel swallowed,
take my hand. Dangle your feet from the fence
when you miss me, and I'll shake all the dust
from the hymnals to name each floating god
-speck after our grandmothers. Don't forget
to water the plants. What's the heart if not
a teapot of blood carried in the chest?

You called me a piano turned over,
and you knew the setting sun was a man
walking toward me who needed firewood
more than he needed song. If the season
whittles us down, hallelujah our spines.
Praise our hollow-bell bodies still ringing.

SELF-PORTRAIT AS HEADLESS JOHN THE BAPTIST HITCHHIKING

God makes more sense this way.

When blood flows from the neck, the body
looks like an uncorked bottle

but maybe this leaves more room for salvation.
The less of me, the less of sin. You said I was temptation,

the way my eyes looked pure as pine
in a window of white, but still called me a saint

after I changed your flat tire. You're right—
holiness is in the hands even if it's always the head

      that gets haloed.

I said I wanted to worship something, even if it's just the black

beetles in your yard crawling around hurriedly
like pieces of a star trying to reassemble itself.

In your apartment we danced like we knew each other.
You rubbed your hands against my neck and shoulder

      as if you were shaping me out of a blackberry vine.

I said the dogmouth dark carried me here and laid me
in your bed. I said *lamb*

and felt myself become gospel in your hands.

LOVE, CIRCULAR SAW BLADE

In the field the last cricket of summer
declared itself the size of my faith, my fever

like a dog's mouth. The bird in the dog's mouth safe
against a tongue with no vocabulary for want. We hold so much

in our mouths, but there's always room for loneliness.

When the holy acre said You too will find your place

between flower and fang, I knew our country was destined
to capsize with nothing but oil to give the sunken garden.

     When we lie down, I am the field and you are the fog.
     Here—I found a corner of the world where scientists

     are still searching the ocean floor for a boat named God,

who will forgive the invasive beetle species
hollowing out the redwoods in the west

before he considers my destructions. I love you.

     I say your name all the time when you're not around
     just to put more of you in the world, but the fruit are growing

teeth. The dogs are running in the field as if it were an opera house
they wanted to burn down. There's this thing   spinning in me.

It could chew through the piano of my childhood, or any other shape
grief hardens into. The boat named God remains unfound,

but there's a small fish trapped inside it,
a blue one, like a heart thirty times too small.

AFTER US, THE FLOOD

After I realize our bodies are chimneys full of rain.
After we shake out the crows roosting there. After

I visit this sanctuary with Noah and Noah's Name
-less Wife, I name her *third dove wreathed in wonder*

weather. I name her *church built*, and built
to be empty. Here, where the animals have names

to tether their drowning bodies to, here where a body
can be a blank—we're holding hands because every temple

we trespass is a mouth hungry for bodies shaped like ours.
Noah's Nameless Wife unties her hair and says *God, will me*

a sail catching wind. I am a burden breaking
water she says. *Is the anchor down? Good* she says.

I'll break the boat in two.

NOAH'S NAMELESS WIFE SEES A GOLDEN BUST
OF JOAN OF ARC

Sometimes we lose a woman to water

+

sometimes to fire.

+

I tell Noah's Nameless Wife that Joan of Arc is the patron saint of WAVES—

+

Women Accepted for Volunteer Emergency Service.

+

It takes four minutes to drown, she says, how long does it take to burn

+

alive?

+

A woman armed with a sword is a saint. A woman with a husband is a smudge.

+

I try to tell her it's not true.

AS LONG AS YOU WANT

the river is high

or the world is sinking   either way

we have permission to be

too much   I threw out your almanac

it said if you see blood   and none of it is yours

trust there is still bleeding to come   I keep imagining God

as having the brass claw feet

of my mother's tub   imagine a country

where you and I kiss before we burn

our battle flags   I was told to bury my dead

but it's the shovel that's underground now

it was an accident I swear   follow me if you can

to understand my father's mind

I wrapped my mother in Christmas lights

and then I fell in love with the way

she shimmered   darling follow me

deep enough into this cave   when our oxygen

runs thin we'll confuse the glowworms

for teeming yellow moons

POEM ENDING WITH ABRAHAM'S SUFFERING

I said I wanted to change my name to Hallelujah
so everyone who climbed a mountain would yell

my name to clouds they'd finally seen the top of.
Kiss me, Hallelujah. Tonight, no one said my name,

though the moon encrusted a white halo on
the graciously indigo sky. Some nights, the sky is everything

it wants, and not just a wall for our fathers
to nail prayers against. Let the starlight harden

to keys in your hands. Let the stars light you lovely
despite your father's resemblance. Tonight, I want to rename

mountains not after the people who climbed them
but their reasons why. I could say, I wanted to quit

but I was halfway up Mount I Could Never Forgive Myself
If I Gave Up Now. Monarch butterflies in their migration

still curve around a mountain flattened hundreds
of centuries ago. If I could name them anything,

I'd call them *the ideal shape of faith.* Even when
the rain softens them to nothing. When the rain gave

me its thousand names, I felt every drop soft as
the lips of my mother, who can saint even the darkest

cloud until we praise it for being the mother of something.
Rain the shape least like the mountain: shape

of submission to gravity.
Daddy, where are we going? asks Isaac.

Abraham says *I will never ask anything
of God again.* A knife in his tunic.

The mountain so sharp
it cuts open the belly of the morning.

ODE

The barns of my childhood are forgetting their shape,
aging like my father with what the years have done

to his hair. They could be little churches if they had
better windows, or if anyone ever prayed in them.

Name one barn Abraham and one barn Isaac,
and watch them sink into each other.

Watch them crumble under the heel of heaven.
Little dilapidations, time does this to us:

comes in the form of wind to run its fingers
through our hair so softly we don't notice our hair

blowing away, unbuttons our shirts and folds them
neatly on the bed. I am trying, I think, to forgive

myself. Now my parents are older. Now all
the barns are eating themselves like sad stars

God gave up on, living out the rest of their lives
in some quiet pasture, sobbing where no one will hear

them. Hungry still for my name written in dust.
If I leave you, if I am not awake when you succumb

finally to the weight of yourself, it's not because
I don't love you. All my childhood I've watched

how your standing becomes settling. For every inch
you sink in the earth, for every nail and horseshoe

turned artifact, there is in me iron, tin, and everything
else that both resists and promises the same gentle collapse.

IV

YOU CALLED ME CASTAWAY AND I CALLED YOU

darling

+

I could believe the soul is a crater—the impact of
your hands on my chest. Fingertips & lips, forest

+

& fire. You taste like cinnamon, or cyanide.

+

My body: bees in a bottle.

+

I've seen a boy go missing inside himself, so I searched for him
in cracked church bells & shot-out lightbulbs.
I found him at the bottom of the lake

+

in my lungs. You pulled him out, but he never looked

+

the same dressed in all those fishhooks.

+

I could say surrender until it sounds like a song
or salve. I could hold your love in my mouth
& make pearls of it.

PALINODE, OR LULLABY WITH LIGHT AND DARK

Sequoias
sequined

under moonlight
and the way

awe
says always

as if
we really could

live
off this.

:::

I'm not saying

it never existed

but it never existed

the way I'm saying.

:::

I meant to say there were too many stars—

the sky was a flag heavy with them.

Your face shone bright under that nation

and I looked because I couldn't look

away, and looking at your hands, you lying

star-ward like a dare to flare out, I woke up

from dreaming two hatchets glimmering in the grass.

:::

> At night we become statues—
> beautiful from any side.
>
> You said every eyeless earth-
> worm throbbing in the dirt
>
> under the house was
> the mind and mouth
>
> of God. Imagine all the
> flowers we've trampled
>
> are growing in paradise,
> ready to forgive us.

:::

> because the road's endlessness
> & coming home alive
>
> both depend on bones
> & their ability to break

into church music
& if the body becomes

a pillar tarnished
with the imprint

of so many careless hands
& if I tell you now

that I've been the evening
yes, I've been that late

& full of flies
if I tell you

the fog for lack of body
must be my grandfather

that we all
disappear

like that
I take it back

:::

Prayer: I hold antlers to my head and my shadow swoons.

Prayer: horses run into the barn and dart out the other end as birds.

Prayer: the sign around the scarecrow's neck   *My kingdom was kindness.*

NOVENAS

archway archway frame me matadorly

my head almost always a pearl

ringing in a bell never a prayer

better to be tangled in all these dream

catchers better to be   batter up

I'm a broken-down ballerina

I have been standing still   you

could light any candle and it would

look just like me especially tomorrow

*

we should try doing all of this again

especially tomorrow I'll put a rose

in my mouth   and gag on it

I mariachi the foals to sleep I let my name

in your mouth leave a gold bite and

say thank you thank you   Virgin Mary

of leaking gunpowder   why won't

the fireworks start   don't leave there's just

enough stars to make a new flag

*

I'm rattling like a clunker isn't it funny

how I see myself most in the women

my father calls insane   I see myself mist

at my best I'm pinned wings and all

for careful scrutiny   at least I'm lovely

I could close the door on every version

of myself that sunbursts out of a revolver

but whose house would that be   and what

if they return as I'm biting into their lemon

NOAH'S NAMELESS WIFE TAKES INVENTORY

horse heart hyena heart swan spine
silver fish shin -ing in black
water yes timber wolf tooth yes
pity the ark with its belly
full of glow -ing tongues
touch the lion's paw only while
it sleeps the red -tailed hawk
with jewels for eyes swallows
the field mouse and the mouse
was the only proof the field
existed what else will be
forgotten the hawk will starve
soon we will starve soon the
dogs will howl like a god
learning the word for light
and nothing will howl back

YOU ARE COUNTING THE WAVES

but numbers don't induce order. Chaos looks
like a lionfish. Malignancy wrapped in a blue sail—

lionfish covered in compass needles: striped fingers
stretching everywhere for their companion.

> You are counting on the universe,
> but it cannot be imagined any other way.

To grab the whisper written in venom, to count

what is without number on fingers meant to writhe
what they touch—hold your breath

and ask this one thing of the world: to keep
the pain fully inside, to let it swell within.

Welcome. Heave.

When you let go, chart the sting

red   and stringy as a constellation: fever
on the chest of heaven. Look: you're a map-reader now.

See if you can tell where your body's going.
Wherever it is, the water will make room for you,

you who are less permanent than the drowned statues
of algae-tinted cities. You will take the ocean in

and give it back

and from your substance will thrive
so many brilliant-colored lionfish.

ALL THAT DAZZLING DAWN HAS PUT ASUNDER: YOU GATHER A LAMB

When you tell the story, you're the fox, quiet as fire but just
as hungry. If you believe this season and all its hunger

has a father, you must forgive yourself for having
his resemblance. Forgive me: I have been trying

to cut the world down to a single sentence.
One with your name in it. Your head is heavy,

a little moon on my shoulder. The laws of absence
say empty space begins where the object ends,

so if the teeth around your door start gnawing,
begin. If you open your eyes and find yourself held

in the mouth of your own feral name, be gone.
Hand me a scythe if you mean the blood

of a past season stains this present one. If you mean
to keep your hands empty, let go of my shirt. Somewhere

tonight, an abandoned mechanical bull is being coddled
by a calf—the ending of every story is about wanting

to be touched. You said Lord, the field is opening
its palm for us. Shadows pulling themselves together

like the redeemed in Christ reassembling their bodies.
And the stars? The stars are doing what they always do.

POEM WITH THREE NAMES OF GOD +
A PROMISE TO MYSELF

for Jon Wright

And in the beginning, I thought my father's hands
looked like old countries, I thought the dried rivers

running through his palms were all that remained
of the land he carried with him. I have been making

a list of the promises my favorite things can and can
not keep. A bridge over the river promises you're not

too heavy. A father promises to eventually be a knot
of electric seconds between synapses called a memory.

Our spines promise to remember their shape, but some
promises break. In the beginning God promised light

but this might have meant fire. God promised his name
but some names break. *Abba* means father, *Elohim*

means something has just been made. A wolf maybe.
A series of rivers to trap it. A group of fathers leaving

because God told them to. My friends are always reminding
me how patient God is. Whether in the form of a sixteenth-

century Mexican church at the bottom of a river
slowly reappearing in the drought season,

or as the diamond my grandmother lost at the edge
of the woods while chopping firewood. How

my mother over and over returned to the tree line
to search on her knees, as if she were trying to unearth

one of *YHWH*'s misplaced names. Maybe handful of wet soil
despite a month of no rain. Maybe red fungal pore that somehow

smears gold under the fingernails. Maybe God lost his name
and whispered sounds until it flew back to him in the dark,

its feathers chewed to shreds from mothers' mouths—
lost diamonds shining in its stomach.

+

One day, strangers will drink water from each other's
cupped hands. We won't call this a miracle. One day,

we'll build a library that lets you borrow birds
instead of books. Don't call this place heaven,

because you'll want everyone to feel welcome.
You can be lost. Like the diamond from a wedding

ring lost to the woods, we'll tell stories about you,
knowing you're somewhere shining. We just

haven't found you yet. One day you'll look
at your open hands and realize how much country

your father gave you. Your rivers. Your dried deltas.
Are you listening? Every bridge you've ever crossed

will eventually collapse, heavy with rust and neglect.
The miracle here is that you weren't standing on any

of them despite your rust. Despite their patience every wolf
you've ever looked in the eyes will eventually be whittled

down by its own hunger until daisies crack open
its chest, and little lost diamond son, there you'll be:

alive enough to hear your name mouthed by any animal
following your scent across your favorite bridge.

NOTES

"Traveler but I scarcely ever listened" is a fragment of Sappho translated by Anne Carson.

"This is plenty. This is more than enough" (in "Sonnet River") is from Geoffrey Hill's "September Song."

"As long as you want" is a fragment of Sappho translated by Anne Carson. The poem with that title is for Rachel Guerry.

"All that dazzling dawn has put asunder" is a fragment of Sappho translated by Anne Carson.

ACKNOWLEDGMENTS

Grateful acknowledgment is offered to the editors of the following journals for publishing these poems, sometimes in earlier versions:

32 Poems
Beloit Poetry Journal
Borderlands: Texas Poetry Review
The Cincinnati Review
Cosmonauts Avenue
Cotton Xenomorph
Feral: A Journal of Poetry and Art
Grist
The Hunger
Ink & Nebula
The Matador Review
Noble / Gas Qtrly
RHINO
Ruminate
The West Review

"Triptych Just Before Mass" was republished in *Verse Daily*.

Some poems have previously appeared in the chapbooks *This Might Have Meant Fire* (Bull City Press, 2019) and *American Cavewall Sonnets* (Bull City Press, 2021), as well as in the anthology *Até Mais: Latinx Futurisms*.

*

Thank you, thank you, my teachers: Marilyn Ford, Kendall Dunkelberg, T. K. Lee, Mary Miller, Randall Horton, L. Lamar Wilson, T. R. Hummer, Jacqueline Tremble, Shayla Lawson.

Thank you, thank you, writers who improved some of these poems in workshops: Celeste Schueler, Lilyanne Kane, Thomas Richardson, Xen Dyl, Allison Chestnut, Dani Putney, Tammie Ward Rice, Jeanna Graves, Ashley Hewitt, Diane Finlayson, Exodus Brownlow, Kathleen Galvin, Beth Kander, Katrina Byrd.

Thank you, thank you, poets who love and share: Beth Gordon, John Dorroh, torrin a. greathouse, Ruben Quesada, CAConrad, Han VanderHart, Kasey Jueds, Ben Niespodziany, Tom Snarsky, Eduardo C. Corral, Jason Myers, Keith S. Wilson, Destiny O. Birdsong, Devin Gael Kelly, Catherine Pierce, Mike Smith, Maia Elgin Wegmann, Paula Harris.

Thank you, thank you, Bull City poets and editors: Ross White, Noah Stetzer, Maria Isabelle Carlos.

Thank you, thank you, Acre Books poets and editors, for helping this book become: Lisa Ampleman, Shara Lessley, and Nicola Mason.

Thank you to my family, Carlos and Haley Salazar, Newton and Melanie Guerry.

Thank you to my sisters and brothers: Rebekah, Ruthe, and Fran, Josh, and Justin,

& Thank you to my resplendent spouse, Rachel Guerry.